What Is Little?

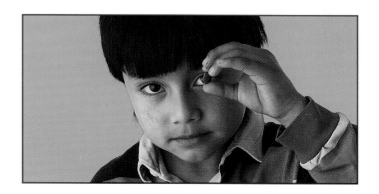

Story and photographs by
Tony Salazar

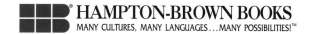
HAMPTON-BROWN BOOKS
MANY CULTURES, MANY LANGUAGES...MANY POSSIBILITIES!™

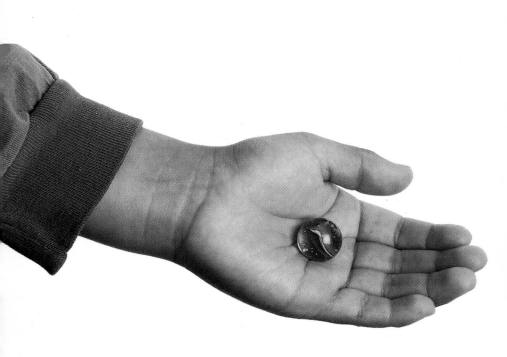

a little marble

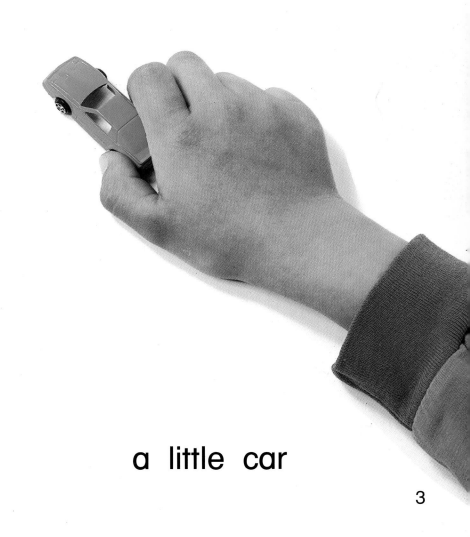

a little car

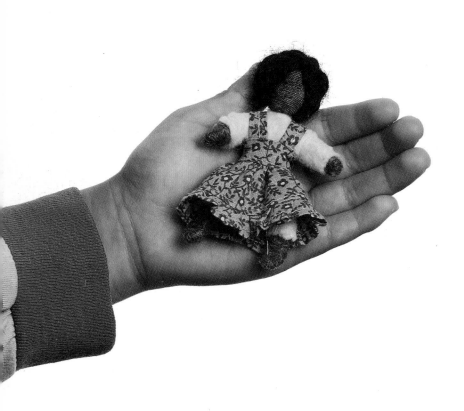

a little doll

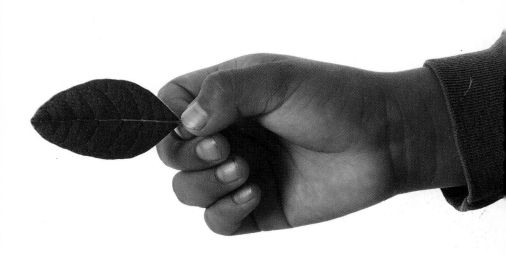

a little leaf

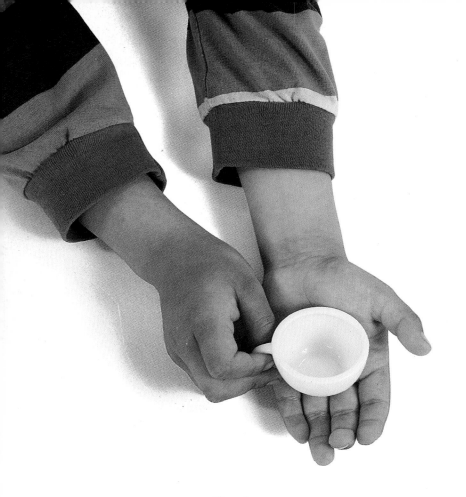

a little cup

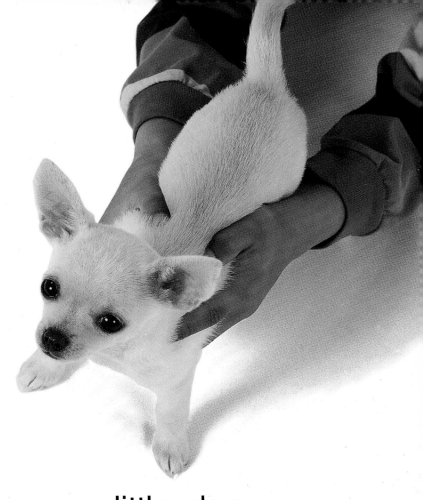

a little dog

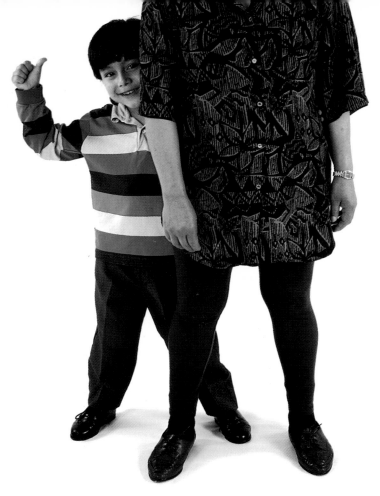

and a little boy!